PATRICIA TEIXEIRA

The Dark Side Behind the Wheel

Contents

1

Thank you

S aying "thank you" feels wholly insufficient for the boundless support my family has provided and the unwavering courage they've instilled in me throughout the journey of writing this book.

To my family…thank you is not enough….

Even though my daughter, Soraia, doesn't share my passion for Formula 1, her unwavering support for my ideas has been a beacon of encouragement - 'I love you'

To my husband Daniel, my steadfast pillar, who fearlessly supports my wildest notions without hesitation—I lack the words to adequately express my gratitude and love. You are my life.

My mom Luzia, always by my side, embracing even the zaniest ideas with a playful spirit, deserves a special mention.

Even from a distance, my mother and father-in-law have consistently been a significant presence in my life, and as always, their unwavering support has been nothing short of amazing.

Beyond my family, there exists a truly exceptional group of individuals who have been by my side throughout this past year.

These are not merely work colleagues; they've become cherished friends who have lent their amazing support in various aspects of my life.

Their encouragement, especially on this incredible journey, means more to me than words can convey.The keen interest they all share in this sport and their excitement about my book were powerful motivators towards its completion.

Claire, Ryan V., Gabriel, Luke C., Alessio, Noel,Kurt, Ralph—your contributions have been immeasurable.

Thank you for everything.

Also, Matthew X., Neil, and Chris A.—when I was at a loss, uncertain about the title or even the cover, you fearlessly stepped in, as you always do.

Another person who deserves my heartfelt gratitude is Melvin C.While he may not have been directly involved in the book project, his incredible support during my HR work was invaluable in my daily life.

To all of you, thank you for believing in me.

2

Why?

ello,my name is Patricia, Formula 1 is not just a
passion; it's a way of life for me. I immerse myself in
the world of F1 as much as possible. My background
is quite diverse, with degrees in Civil Engineering and HR with
Psychology.

One aspect of Formula 1 that often weighs on my mind is the
immense stress that drivers endure, especially as they become
public figures. It's disheartening to witness the prevalence of
racism, hate, and negativity on social media directed towards
the drivers and teams. Such online hostility can cause significant harm.

This book serves as an alert and a call to action. It aims to raise
awareness about the challenges faced by drivers and teams, but
most importantly, it emphasizes the importance of empathy
and respect from fans like myself. At the end of the day, the
individuals responsible for the teams and the drivers are, above
all, human beings with their own emotions and vulnerabilities

Remember, treating others as you would want to be treated goes a long way in creating a more supportive and compassionate environment in the world of Formula 1.

Team Work

3

The Flagman Casts the Green: Unveiling the Mental Struggles in Formula 1 Racing

In the heart of the stadium, the cacophonous symphony of roaring engines reverberated through the air as a kaleidoscope of cars, resplendent in hues of red, yellow, and blue, tore down the track with an ear-splitting intensity. Their tires clung tenaciously to the asphalt as they vied for supremacy, each driver pushing the limits in pursuit of the coveted finish line.

This high-speed spectacle, a fervent crowd erupted in jubilation, their cheers and exhortations echoing throughout the venue. The drivers, displaying audacious precision with every turn and exhibiting a level of skill honed through years of relentless practice, piloted their machines as though they were extensions of themselves. This seamless choreography bore testament to the exhaustive training and unwavering dedication invested in both car and driver alike.

Nevertheless, beyond the glitz and glamour of Formula 1 racing lies a somber and often concealed aspect—one fraught with mental health challenges, particularly among the sport's younger participants. While the world marvels at the audacity, precision, and prowess of these athletes, few are privy to the emotional and psychological battles that have shadowed them from the sport's inception.

The pressures faced by Formula 1 drivers, especially those who embark on their careers at a tender age, are nothing short of monumental. Thrust into the limelight, their lives are subjected to relentless scrutiny by the media, with every move dissected by an expectant global audience. The pursuit of victory offers little respite, as they become ensnared in an unrelenting quest for excellence that knows no bounds.

Navigating the high-speed world of racing frequently isolates these young drivers from their families and support networks, forcing them into a nomadic existence on the global racing circuit. Loneliness and isolation become constant companions, exacerbated by grueling hours of training and travel that leave precious little time for nurturing meaningful relationships outside the realm of the sport.

The ever-present specter of injury or even mortality casts a long shadow over the world of Formula 1, a constant reminder of the perilous nature of their chosen profession. The loss of colleagues and friends in tragic accidents often leaves survivors grappling with the twin burdens of survivor's guilt and an ever-looming awareness of their own vulnerability.

Financial pressures further compound the mental health struggles of young drivers, as sponsorship deals and team contracts are intricately tied to performance. The fear of financial instability can become an oppressive weight on their minds. The relentless pursuit of success, in its most unforgiving form, can push them to the brink, leading to burnout and despair.

In their relentless pursuit of perfection, drivers are required to adhere to stringent physical regimens, rendering them susceptible to the physical toll exacted by the sport. Injuries and the associated pain can intensify the emotional burden they bear, further exacerbating their mental health challenges.

Historically, the culture of Formula 1 has discouraged open discourse about mental health. Drivers have been conditioned to project an image of invincibility, concealing their vulnerabilities behind a veneer of stoicism. This culture of silence has posed formidable barriers to young drivers seeking help or support for their mental health concerns, perpetuating their silent suffering.

Recent years, however, have seen a burgeoning awareness of the significance of mental health within the Formula 1 sphere. Teams and organizations have begun acknowledging the formidable challenges faced by their drivers, and they are now implementing comprehensive programs to support their mental well-being. The aspiration is to shatter the entrenched silence surrounding mental health, enabling young drivers to access the assistance and resources they require to navigate the arduous landscape of Formula 1 while safeguarding their mental equilibrium.

In summation, the enigmatic underbelly of Formula 1 racing, characterized by the specter of depression among its young drivers, has remained a persistent issue since the sport's inception. The exacting nature of their profession, coupled with isolation, the ever-present specter of tragedy, financial pressures, the physical toll, and a culture of silence, has left an indelible mark on the mental health of these athletes. It is of paramount importance that the racing community continues to confront these challenges, providing young drivers with the necessary support and resources to navigate the demanding terrain of Formula 1 while preserving their mental well-being.

4

The Intricate Tapestry of Formula 1: Triumphs, Tragedies, and Evolution

Formula 1, a storied motor sport spectacle, is a rich tapestry woven with tales of glorious triumphs and heart-wrenching tragedies. It has metamorphosed from a niche amateur racing series into the apex of motor racing, graced by legendary drivers whose names are etched in the annals of racing history.

The genesis of Formula 1, commonly referred to as F1, dates back to the year 1950 when the inaugural race was held at the iconic Silverstone circuit in England. The formal inception of the championship followed in 1958, marked by the triumph of Argentine driver Juan Manuel Fangio, who clinched the inaugural driver's title. Over the decades, Formula 1 has undergone a remarkable evolution, with an ever-expanding roster of teams and drivers participating in each season.

Presently, it comprises 20 teams and 20 drivers, all vying for the coveted title of the year's champion.

Formula 1 drivers epitomize the epitome of talent and dedication in the world of sports. They must possess a unique blend of skill, courage, and composure to compete at the pinnacle of motor sport.

Drivers navigate the complexities of each track layout while meticulously devising race strategies, all while managing the immense pressure and expectations from their teams and the ever-watchful media. These drivers are not just athletes; they are also the sport's ambassadors, responsible for crafting and maintaining their public image and marketability.

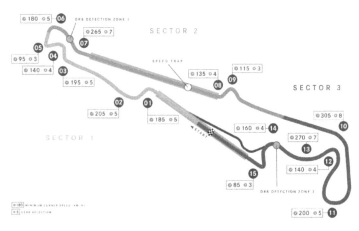

Circuit Paul Ricard - French Grand Prix

In the realm of Formula 1, the teams represent the zenith of engineering excellence. They harness cutting-edge technology and innovative design principles to craft cars that are both exceptionally fast and reliably durable. Teams motor sport meticulously to accumulate maximum race points, ultimately vying for championship titles.

Media coverage has been an integral part of Formula 1 since its inception.

The landscape has transformed from traditional newspapers and television broadcasts to encompass the digital realm. Social media, in particular, has emerged as a vital component of the sport, enabling real-time interaction between drivers, teams, and fans. This heightened engagement on social platforms has exponentially expanded Formula 1's global audience, elevating its popularity and marketability to unprecedented heights.

Competition in Formula 1 is not limited to the racetrack; it extends to the quest for fame and recognition. As the sport has grown, rivalries among teams and drivers have intensified, resulting in exhilarating on-track battles and off-track dramas, including intense disputes and occasional clashes.

Recent years have witnessed the sport becoming even more fiercely competitive with innovations such as the "Double Points" system introduced in 2014 and the addition of "fastest lap" bonus points in 2020. These changes have amplified the stakes, compelling teams and drivers to seek every possible advantage to secure a championship victory.

The 2021 Formula 1 season marked a watershed moment with the debut of the Abu Dhabi Grand Prix as the season's grand finale. It delivered a breathtaking climax to the year, with Lewis Hamilton and Red Bull Racing emerging as the champions. The season also saw the implementation of stringent regulations by the Fédération Internationale de l'Automobile (FIA), including rigorous track limit enforcement and penalties for unsafe driving, intensifying the level of competition.

Abu Dhabi Grand Prix 2021

The 2021 season unfolded as a captivating saga, replete with remarkable performances and heartrending setbacks. From its inaugural race to the climactic conclusion, it was a relentless battle for supremacy among the top teams and drivers, all pushing their limits to gain a decisive edge over their adversaries. Ultimately, Lewis Hamilton and Red Bull Racing etched their names in the pantheon of motor sport greatness.

Formula 1 is an ever-evolving sport, shaped by the collective efforts of teams, drivers, and fervent fans. The advent of social media has enhanced engagement and interaction, extending the sport's reach. The 2021 season of Formula 1 proved to be a spellbinding chapter, replete with unforgettable races and performances, culminating in the iconic Abu Dhabi finale. As the sport continues its dynamic evolution, the future of Formula 1 promises to be as enthralling and unpredictable as its storied past.

5

Formula One: A Prestigious Racing Championship

F ormula One, often referred to as F1, stands as the preeminent echelon of single-seater auto racing, operating under the auspices of the Fédération Internationale de l'Automobile (FIA). The FIA World Championship for Drivers was inaugurated in 1950, while the World Constructors' Championship was introduced in 1958.

The term "Formula" in its nomenclature alludes to a stringent set of regulations governing the design and specifications of participating cars. A Formula One season encompasses a succession of races, known as Grands Prix (French for "grand prizes" or "great victories"), conducted across the globe, spanning purpose-built F1 circuits and public roads.

The results of each race are assessed via a points system to ascertain two prestigious annual World Championships: one for drivers and the other for constructors. At season's end, the driver and constructor accumulating the most points are bestowed with the esteemed titles of World Champions.

Ferrari, founded by the Italian racing luminary Enzo Ferrari in 1929, enjoys an illustrious position in the annals of Formula 1 history. Since the sport's inception in 1950, Ferrari has emerged as a dominant force, securing an impressive tally of 16 constructors' championships and 15 drivers' championships, making it the most successful team in Formula 1 history in terms of championship victories. Ferrari boasts an extensive heritage in motor sport, renowned for its high-performance vehicles and distinctive red livery. The team commands a devoted and impassioned fan base, solidifying its status as one of the sport's most prestigious and esteemed entities.

Mercedes, a formidable contender in recent Formula 1 history, clinched seven consecutive Constructors' Championships from 2014 to 2020. The team also secured four Drivers' Championships with the remarkable Lewis Hamilton, who consistently ranks among the sport's foremost drivers. Mercedes employs cutting-edge technology and engineering prowess in crafting its cars, maintaining an unwavering commitment to innovation and relentless improvement. The team's triumphant track record serves as a testament to its relentless pursuit of excellence.

Williams, established in 1977 by Sir Frank Williams, boasts a storied history of success in Formula 1, amassing nine Constructors' Championships and seven Drivers' Championships. Williams has perennially ranked among the sport's top echelons and has fostered young talent development. In recent years, however, the team has faced challenges in maintaining its competitive edge, with its last race victory dating back to 2012. Nevertheless, Williams endures as one of the most revered and accomplished outfits in Formula 1 history, retaining a pivotal role in the sport.

As of the 2021 Formula One season, 34 World Championship drivers' titles and 30 World Championship constructors' titles have been conferred.

The past decade in Formula 1 has witnessed a dynamic series of transformations and milestones. To provide a glimpse of the drivers who clinched the Formula 1 World Championship in the last decade:

2012: Sebastian Vettel (Red Bull Racing)
  2013: Sebastian Vettel (Red Bull Racing)
  2014: Lewis Hamilton (Mercedes)
  2015: Lewis Hamilton (Mercedes)
  2016: Nico Rosberg (Mercedes)
  2017: Lewis Hamilton (Mercedes)
  2018: Lewis Hamilton (Mercedes)
  2019: Lewis Hamilton (Mercedes)
  2020: Lewis Hamilton (Mercedes)
  2021: Max Verstappen (Red Bull Racing)
  2022: Max Verstappen (Red Bull Racing)

The inaugural Formula 1 race materialized on May 13th, 1950, at Silverstone Circuit in Northampton shire. The victor of this historic race was Italian driver Giuseppe Farina, who piloted an Alfa Romeo 159 with a top speed of 140 km/h.

The escalating costs of competing in Formula One precipitated a decline in the number of entries from independent teams, and by 1963, private teams that could meet the escalating financial demands were the sole contenders. Escalating costs and the challenge of upholding parity with factory-supported teams contributed to the withdrawal of factory teams like BR.

Throughout Formula 1's storied history, several iconic and widely recognized drivers have left indelible marks on the sport:

Michael Schumacher: A seven-time World Champion, Schumacher is hailed as one of the greatest Formula 1 drivers in history, with a record 91 Grand Prix victories spanning 14 seasons.

Lewis Hamilton: A seven-time World Champion, Hamilton stands as the most successful driver in Formula 1 history in terms of race wins and World Championships, boasting a record 96 Grand Prix wins.

Ayrton Senna: A three-time World Champion, Senna is celebrated as one of the most gifted and iconic drivers in Formula 1 annals, tallying 41 Grand Prix victories.

Juan Manuel Fangio: A five-time World Champion, Fangio ranks among the most illustrious drivers in motor sport history, amassing 24 Grand Prix victories and setting numerous records.

Alain Prost: A four-time World Champion, Prost is venerated as one of the most accomplished and iconic drivers in Formula 1 history, boasting 51 Grand Prix wins.

Formula 1 has not been immune to tragedy, with notable fatalities involving drivers, team members, and track marshals.

Some poignant moments include:

Jules Bianchi's story is one that I've come to view with a deep sense of respect and emotion. The way he glided through tracks, his cherubic smile lighting up the pit lane, and his undeniable talent made him stand out as a beacon of hope for the future of motor sport. His racing wasn't merely an outcome of an inherited legacy, it felt as if it was an extension of his very being, a reflection of his soul. Every race, every lap he took, he showcased a grace and dedication that earned him not just the respect of his contemporaries but also the undying adoration of fans across the globe.

Yet, the fateful day in 2014 during the Japanese Grand Prix remains etched in the memories of all who love the sport. The crash was a brutal reminder of the unpredictability and inherent dangers of racing. Jules sustained grave injuries, and the world, especially the motor sport community, prayed, wished, and hoped against hope for his recovery. But the tragic news in 2015 confirmed our worst fears, and the void left by his passing is something words might never be able to describe adequately.

Recalling Jules' journey brings to the forefront the dichotomies that exist in the world of motorsport. The exhilaration, the thrill of speed, and the glorious victories stand in stark contrast to the potential dangers that loom at every corner. Yet, in Jules' memory, we don't only see a tale of tragedy. His life and his career stand as enduring symbols of human resilience, unyielding passion, and an unwavering commitment to chasing one's dreams, regardless of the obstacles.

His legacy teaches us invaluable lessons: to cherish each moment, to chase our dreams with fervor and genuine love, and to always recognize and respect the fragility of life. Jules might not be with us today, but the imprints of his journey, his spirit, and his dedication to the sport continue to inspire many, myself included.

Jules Bianchi

<u>Roland Ratzenberger,</u> a name that resonates profoundly within the annals of motorsport history. The Austrian racer embodied the spirit of a true racer: tenacious, passionate, and dedicated to the craft. Every time he took to the track, he showcased a unique blend of skill and determination that was evident to all who watched him race.

However, it's impossible to recall Ratzenberger's name without a heavy heart. In 1994, during the qualifying session for the San Marino Grand Prix, a catastrophic accident claimed his life. That weekend in Imola is remembered as one of the darkest in Formula 1's history, a somber reminder of the immense risks these drivers take each time they step into their cars.

Ratzenberger's tragic passing came just a day before the race in which the sport lost another icon, Ayrton Senna. The juxtaposition of these two immense losses within such a short span brought the motor sport world to its knees. It forced the racing community to confront the very real and ever-present dangers of the sport, leading to significant changes in safety protocols and regulations to protect drivers.

Yet, when we remember Roland Ratzenberger, it shouldn't just be in the context of his untimely passing. While that moment serves as a reminder of the sport's unpredictability, Ratzenberger's legacy is so much more. He was a beacon of hope for many aspiring racers, exemplifying what it means to chase a dream with unwavering determination. He rose through the ranks, facing numerous challenges along the way, but never let them deter him from his passion for racing.

In my reflections on Roland, I choose to remember him for the racer he was, the dreams he chased, and the indelible mark he left on the sport. His journey serves as a poignant reminder to live our lives with purpose, passion, and an unyielding drive. Even though he is no longer with us, the memories of his races, his dedication, and his spirit continue to inspire and motivate many in the motor sport world and beyond.

Roland Ratzenberger

Tom Pryce, a name etched in the heart of motor sport history, was a shining star of British racing. Hailing from Wales, Pryce's journey in the world of racing was nothing short of meteoric. With a natural flair for the sport, his style was both smooth and aggressive, making him a formidable presence on the track. Each race he participated in was testament to his profound dedication and raw talent.

However, the unpredictability and inherent danger of motor sport became painfully evident in 1977. During the South African Grand Prix, a sequence of tragic events unfolded that led to an accident, ultimately claiming Pryce's life. That day, the world lost not just an exceptional talent, but a spirited soul whose passion for racing was evident in every turn and every lap he drove.

The accident that took Tom's life was one of those horrifying moments that serves as a brutal reminder of the razor-thin margin between life and death in high-speed sports like Formula 1. It shook the foundation of the motor sport community and led to a renewed focus on safety measures, ensuring that the sacrifices made by drivers like Pryce were not in vain.

But beyond the tragedy, Tom Pryce's legacy is one of inspiration. In his short career, he showcased the essence of what it means to be a racer: the unyielding determination, the pursuit of excellence, and the sheer joy of being behind the wheel. Stories of his humility off the track and his prowess on it continue to inspire generations of racers and fans alike.

Tom Pryce

Until today, the memory of Ayrton Senna's tragic crash continues to weigh heavily on my heart. To honor his legacy and to remind myself of the immense risks that all Formula 1 drivers undertake, I've chosen to keep a distant photo of that fateful moment.

Ayrton Senna crash moment

Forever Ayrton Senna, a legend whose indomitable spirit and passion for racing will always be etched in our hearts.

In their memory, Formula 1 has continually evolved its safety standards, pushing the boundaries of engineering and innovation to reduce the risks faced by drivers. The sacrifices made by these fallen heroes have spurred the sport to enhance safety measures, ensuring that their legacy lives on in a safer and more secure Formula 1.

While these drivers may have left us prematurely, their enduring legacy serves as a poignant reminder of the profound impact of motor sport on the human spirit. They are the embodiment of the daring spirit of Formula 1, and their legend lives on in the hearts and minds of fans and racers alike, inspiring us all to push the limits and chase our dreams, no matter the obstacles in our path.

Throughout its captivating history, Formula 1 has borne witness to numerous momentous events and milestones:

1950: The inaugural Formula 1 World Championship race at Silverstone Circuit in England on May 13, 1950, saw Giuseppe Farina secure victory in an Alfa Romeo.

1961: Phil Hill made history by becoming the first American driver to clinch the Formula 1 World Championship.

1976: James Hunt triumphed in a dramatic season finale at the Japanese Grand Prix, winning the Formula 1 World Championship. The season's climax pitted Hunt against Niki Lauda, who had miraculously recovered from a life-threatening crash earlier in the season.

Niki Lauda & James Hunt

2008: Lewis Hamilton etched his name in history as the first driver of African and Caribbean descent to capture the Formula 1 World Championship.

Lewis Hamilton won his first Formula 1 World Championship in 2008, driving for McLaren. He became the youngest ever World Champion at the time, a record which has since been surpassed by Sebastian Vettel in 2010. Moreover, Hamilton's victory did indeed mark a significant moment as he is of African and Caribbean descent (his father is from Grenada, and his maternal grandparents are from Grenada and England). Over the years, Hamilton has often spoken about the importance of diversity in the sport and has been an advocate for change within the motor sport community.

2014: Mercedes-AMG Petronas Formula One Team secured its maiden Formula 1 World Constructors' Championship title.

2020: The COVID-19 pandemic disrupted the Formula 1 calendar, resulting in the postponement or cancellation of several races. The season eventually resumed with a series of "double-header" events, where two races were held at the same venue on consecutive weekends.

On one hand, there's the glitz, glamour, and the thrilling spectacle of cars racing at breakneck speeds. The shimmering tracks in locales from Monaco to Singapore, the roaring crowds, and the podium champagne are all hallmarks of a sport steeped in luxury and excitement.

Yet, behind the visor, within the confines of the cockpit, and even in the quieter moments away from the track, there lies a contrasting reality. A reality where the weight of expectation presses heavily on shoulders that bear the hopes of millions. The rigorous physical training, the countless hours of practice, strategy planning, and the knowledge that a fraction of a second could be the difference between victory and defeat - these are burdens that every driver and team member must bear.

Every decision, every move is dissected by pundits, fans, and critics alike. In this age of social media, even a minor mistake can be magnified, leading to a torrent of criticism. It's not just about driving fast; it's about navigating the intricate maze of team dynamics, sponsor expectations, media engagements, and personal aspirations.

In such an environment, mental well-being can often take a backseat. The adrenaline and focus on the next race might mask the creeping tendrils of stress, anxiety, or depression. As fans and observers, it's easy to forget that beneath the helmets and behind the steering wheels are humans with emotions, fears, and vulnerabilities.

The racing community is gradually waking up to the importance of addressing mental health head-on. But there's still a long way to go. Drivers need support systems that extend beyond physical fitness and technical acumen. Teams should foster environments where drivers and staff feel safe to express their feelings and seek help without fear of judgment.

We, as fans, also play a crucial role. Our support should be unwavering, not just in victory but in defeat. Our admiration should be for the person as much as for the driver. By creating a more understanding and compassionate F1 community, we can ensure that our beloved sport remains not only a showcase of speed and skill but also of empathy and humanity.

In the roaring, pulsating heart of Formula 1, where speed is worshipped and risks are taken at every turn, the quiet introduction of the Halo cockpit protection device whispers a tale of profound care and deep reverence for human life. It's not just a technical advancement; it's an embrace, a protective hand that promises safety amidst the chaos.

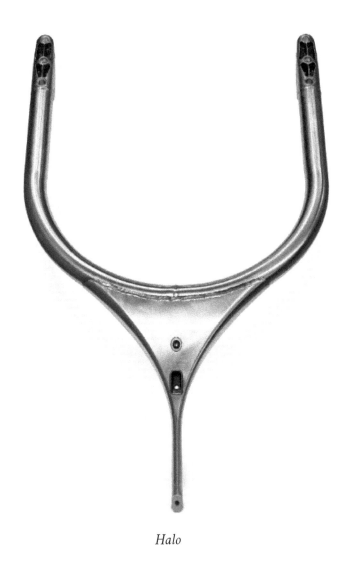

Halo

When the Halo, a graceful arc perched above the cockpit,

first graced the racetracks, it was met with mixed emotions. Some saw it as an intrusion on the sport's aesthetics; others, a necessary evolution. But its real worth is not in its design or appearance, but in the precious lives it safeguards.

More than just physical protection, the Halo offers something invaluable: peace of mind. Racing, a relentless dance with danger, demands more than just skill and speed; it calls for courage, every single time. And with the Halo standing sentinel, drivers can push the boundaries, knowing there's a guardian watching over them.

As we immerse ourselves in the thrill of each race, let's take a moment to appreciate the silent hero - the Halo. It stands as a symbol of Formula 1's heart, a reminder that amidst the pursuit of glory, the sport tenderly cradles the lives of its stars, ensuring they race not just with passion, but with a promise of protection.

The Halo isn't just a feature; it's a gentle, powerful testament to Formula 1's commitment to its drivers, an emblem of love in a world driven by speed.

British Grand Prix 2022

Zhou Guanyu, the driver who experienced a harrowing crash during the 2022 British Grand Prix, has expressed his amazement at surviving the incident. He credits the Halo device with saving his life.

6

Mental Resilience and the Fight against Depression

Formula 1, synonymous with roaring engines and blistering speeds, represents the pinnacle of motor sport. But beneath the glamour and adrenaline lies a critical challenge that often escapes public attention:

The Immense Pressure of Formula 1 Racing

Performance Pressure: Every time drivers step into an F1 car, they are acutely aware that their every move is scrutinized. A fraction of a second can be the difference between pole position and a mid-grid start. Such extreme expectations can breed stress and, eventually, manifest into more severe conditions like depression.

Life at Stake: Racing at speeds surpassing 200 mph, the risk is a constant companion. This looming danger, coupled with the need for split-second decisions, creates a unique and constant mental strain.

Off-Track Challenges: The demand isn't limited to the racetrack. Balancing sponsor obligations, team expectations, media appearances, and personal life, drivers often find little respite from stressors, increasing vulnerability to mental health challenges.

Unforgiving Nature of Competition:Formula 1 is the pinnacle of motorsports, where split-second decisions matter and the pressure is immense. While victories bring unmatched glory, the consistent inability to perform is intensely scrutinized. This constant spotlight can lead drivers to doubt their abilities. Feeling like they've let down their team or fans can be isolating, even leading to stress and, in severe cases, depression. But it's not just drivers; the entire team feels this pressure. In the fast-paced world of F1, understanding and supporting mental well-being is as crucial as chasing that next win.

The Weight of Public Scrutiny: Living under the spotlight, drivers face incessant critique, not just from experts but from a global fan base. Continuous negative feedback can amplify any self-doubt, magnifying mental health issues.

The Path Forward: A Holistic Approach to Driver Welfare

Cultivating Openness: The first step is to dismantle the stigma surrounding mental health in F1. Encouraging drivers to vocalize their struggles can pave the way for early intervention and support.

Resources and Professional Support: Teams have a pivotal role by integrating mental health professionals into their support staff, ensuring drivers have ready access to counseling and guidance.

Physical and Mental Preparedness: Beyond the usual rigorous physical training, drivers should undergo mental resilience training. Techniques like mindfulness meditation, visualization, and cognitive behavioral strategies can be powerful tools in a driver's arsenal.

Beyond the Track: A harmonious work-life balance is imperative. Drivers should be encouraged to disconnect from racing periodically, immersing themselves in hobbies, leisure, and personal pursuits to recharge mentally.

In acknowledging and addressing mental health's vital significance, Formula 1 can pave the way not just for happier athletes but for a more compassionate sporting world. The path to the podium should not come at the cost of one's mental well-being.

Pit Stop

Cultivating Openness in Formula 1's Mental Health Landscape

Understanding the Current Scenario: Historically, the sporting world has celebrated physical prowess and stoicism, often sidelining discussions about mental health. Such an environment can inadvertently foster a culture where individuals feel compelled to mask their struggles, fearing judgment or professional repercussions.

Dismantling Stigma: The stigma surrounding mental health isn't exclusive to F1; it's a societal challenge. However, in a high-pressure environment like F1, this stigma can be particularly detrimental. If drivers believe they'll be perceived as "weak" or "less dedicated" for admitting to mental health challenges, they're less likely to seek help, exacerbating their issues. Addressing this requires a shift in perspective at all levels – from team managers and fellow drivers to media personnel and fans.

The Power of Vocalization: When a prominent figure in the F1 community openly discusses their mental health, it has a two-fold impact. Firstly, it sends a message to other drivers that they're not alone in their struggles. Secondly, it educates the larger community about the genuine pressures drivers face, fostering empathy and understanding.

Early Intervention and Support: By creating an environment where drivers feel comfortable sharing their struggles, teams can identify potential issues early. This proactive approach allows for timely intervention, be it counseling, therapy, or other forms of support, reducing the risk of a driver's mental health deteriorating further.

Role of Teams and Governing Bodies: Teams, sponsors, and governing bodies like the FIA play a crucial role in cultivating openness. They can initiate programs that emphasize mental health's importance, offer training sessions to educate all members about recognizing signs of mental health issues, and implement systems ensuring drivers' confidentiality and support when they come forward with their struggles.

Life at Stake: The Psychological Weight of Racing at Extreme Speeds

The thrill of Formula 1 (F1) comes, in part, from the intense speeds at which the drivers race. However, what often gets lost in the spectacle is the immense psychological burden that these speeds impose on the drivers. Let's break down the "Life at Stake" aspect of F1 racing in detail.

Understanding the Physical Reality: Formula 1 cars are engineering marvels capable of reaching speeds of over 200 mph (322 km/h). At such velocities, everything happens in a blur. The margin for error shrinks dramatically, meaning a minor misjudgment or a slight hiccup in car performance can lead to catastrophic outcomes. The physical danger is not merely a possibility; it is an inherent part of the job.

The Cognitive Load: At these high speeds, drivers have milliseconds to process information and react. Whether it's deciding to overtake, adjusting to changing track conditions, or responding to potential mechanical issues, the cognitive demands are immense. They must continuously process a stream of information from the car, the track, their team, and their own senses, synthesizing it all into optimal decisions in real-time.

Emotional Toll of Potential Harm: Beyond the immediate cognitive challenges, drivers are acutely aware of the risks they face. Every time they strap into their cars, they confront the reality that they are placing their lives on the line. This awareness, even if pushed to the back of their minds during a race, creates an emotional weight that they carry with them.

Impact on Family and Close Ones: The danger also extends its shadow over drivers' families and close friends. Knowing that a loved one is regularly in a high-risk situation can cause significant stress and worry for those close to the driver, which can, in turn, add to the driver's own psychological strain.

Reliance on Split-second Decisions: In many sports, players have the luxury of time, even if it's just a few seconds, to make decisions. In F1, there's often no such luxury. A split-second delay in braking, turning, or accelerating can result in an accident. This necessity for instantaneous decision-making, knowing that lives might be at stake, creates a unique type of mental pressure that few outside the sport can truly understand.

The Aftermath of Incidents: Even with all safety precautions, accidents do happen in F1. Whether a driver is directly involved or merely witnesses a crash, the psychological aftermath can be significant. The memory of a severe accident can linger, potentially affecting a driver's confidence, focus, and overall mental well-being.

Off-Track Challenges

Formula 1 drivers face immense pressures, not just on the track but off it. They wear multiple hats: athletes on the circuit and brand ambassadors off it.

Sponsor commitments can be grueling, involving tight schedules for events, endorsements, and media engagements.

Additionally, harmonious relationships with their teams are pivotal. It's not just about race day performance; it's strategy discussions, debriefs, and fostering team camaraderie, aware that team dynamics can be career-defining.

Moreover, the media spotlight is relentless. Regular press conferences, interviews, and handling tough critiques, especially after underwhelming races, exert psychological strain. Balancing these demands with personal life, where they juggle travel with family time, friendships, and self-care, adds complexity.

Consequently, while F1's track speeds and competition are intense, off-track obligations weave an equally intricate web of challenges, accentuating the sport's mental rigor.

Formula 1, being one of the premier motor sport series globally, garners vast media attention. The immense scrutiny can either be a driver's boon or bane, often shaping perceptions, careers, and legacies.

Post-Race Interviews: Right after a race, adrenaline is still pumping, and emotions are raw. Drivers are often put on the spot with probing questions. For instance, after the controversial collision between Lewis Hamilton and Max Verstappen at the 2021 British Grand Prix, both drivers faced a barrage of questions, with the media dissecting their every word, intensifying the rivalry narrative.

The anguish experienced by the drivers is not the allure that draws me to this sport. Sure, there have been times of frustration, but can we squarely place the blame on either the drivers or the teams? It's essential to remember that these drivers, at the heart of it all, are humans. Their highs and lows resonate deeply, but they shouldn't be the sole focus of our fandom or critique. Let's appreciate the sport while respecting the humanity of all its participants.

Press Conferences: Scheduled press events are platforms where drivers can be asked anything, from technical race details to personal life queries. In 2016, Lewis Hamilton faced criticism for using Snapchat during a press conference in Japan. The media spotlight can be so relentless that sometimes even offhand actions become big news.

Social Media: While not traditional media, the immediate and pervasive nature of social platforms has intensified the media's effect. Pierre Gasly's demotion from Red Bull Racing to Toro Rosso (now Scuderia AlphaTauri) in 2019 led to a media frenzy, with many fans and pundits weighing in on social platforms, turning a professional decision into a major media event.

2019 was a whirlwind year for Pierre Gasly, filled with the highs and lows that remind us of the human side of Formula 1.

Pierre, young and ambitious, started the year with a dream opportunity. He was promoted from Toro Rosso, essentially the "younger sibling" team, to Red Bull Racing, a top-tier team. Think of it as moving from the junior varsity team to the big leagues. With that came immense pressure; he was now teammate to Max Verstappen, a prodigious talent making waves in F1.

Sadly, dreams don't always go as planned. The Red Bull car, intricate and high-strung like a finely-tuned violin, seemed tailor-made for Max. Pierre, despite his best efforts, felt like he was constantly wrestling with it. Imagine trying to dance gracefully with shoes that don't fit.

As the races went by, the strain started showing. He was in the limelight, with every move analyzed. It's like having your struggles broadcasted for the world to judge, all while trying to keep up with the prodigy next door.

Mid-season, Red Bull made a tough call. They moved Pierre back to Toro Rosso and brought in rookie Alexander Albon.

For Pierre, it might've felt like a demotion. But sometimes, home is where you find your rhythm again. Back in familiar territory, Pierre found his mojo. He raced with heart, culminating in a breathtaking P2 finish in Brazil. That podium wasn't just about the trophy; it was a testament to resilience.

Pierre's 2019 story reminds us: F1 isn't just machines and strategies. It's human stories of dreams, challenges, and comebacks.

Seasonal Narratives: The media tends to latch onto narratives, perpetuating them throughout a season or even careers. Nico Rosberg and Lewis Hamilton's intra-team rivalry while at Mercedes was a focal point for several seasons, with their every interaction being meticulously analyzed, sometimes overshadowing the broader championship narrative.

Once upon a time in the world of racing, two friends, Nico and Lewis, raced under the sun, their dreams as vast as the skies. Little did they know that their journey would be more than just rubber on tarmac; it would be under the relentless lens of millions, magnified by social media's voracious appetite.

2014: As they began competing head-to-head in Mercedes, every move was scrutinized. A simple overtaking maneuver was no longer just a racing incident; it was a trending topic. The collision at the Belgian Grand Prix didn't just echo on the racetrack; it reverberated across Twitter threads, Instagram stories, and Facebook debates. Friendships strained under the weight of public opinion.

2015: The spotlight grew harsher. Their dynamic, once about mutual respect, was now fodder for memes, gifs, and viral videos. Each misstep, real or perceived, became a hashtag. The invisible pressure of social media was a third contender in their rivalry.

2016: The Spanish Grand Prix felt like a Shakespearean tragedy played out in 280 characters. Their crash became an emblem of their deteriorating relationship.By Abu Dhabi, when tactics and emotions ran high, it wasn't just a championship on the line; it was personal narratives shaped by countless tweets and posts.

Then, when Nico announced his retirement, social media

erupted. Some praised, some questioned, and others mourned. It wasn't just about a driver hanging up his boots; it was about a person trying to find peace amidst the digital cacophony.

In the Rosberg-Hamilton tale, the tracks and tires were just one part. The unyielding gaze of social media, with its power to judge and influence, played a silent yet potent role. Their story is a testament to the challenges of modern-day sportsmanship, where athletes race not just against each other but against the tidal wave of public sentiment, constantly ebbing and flowing in the vast sea of the internet.

Beyond the glitz and glamour, the engines and the podiums, the Rosberg-Hamilton saga was a human story. It was about two dreamers who once stood together, only to find themselves at crossroads, torn between ambition and a bond that once was. It serves as a poignant reminder of the personal sacrifices and emotional roller-coasters sportsmen endure in the quest for greatness.

Personal Struggles: Drivers' personal challenges are often thrust into the limelight. Romain Grosjean's horrifying crash in the 2020 Bahrain Grand Prix led to extensive media coverage. While the coverage highlighted the safety of modern F1 cars, it also served as a constant reminder of the near-fatal incident, which could add mental pressure to the already shaken driver.

In summary, while media attention is par for the course in elite sports, the relentless nature of the spotlight in F1 magnifies every triumph, mistake, or personal challenge. Drivers are not only racing on the track but also navigating the intricate maze of media narratives and public perceptions.

7

Beyond the Driver's Seat

In the rhythmic heartbeat beneath the visors and the anxious breath behind the gloves lies an undeniable truth: Formula 1, at its essence, is a profound symphony of human passion and ambition. While the roar of the engines might often drown out the subtler tales, those quieter stories resonate with the dedication and dreams of individuals who've poured their souls into the sport.

The pitstop, that fleeting moment in the timeline of a race, carries within it the collective hopes and fears of an entire team. Today's digital age, with its magnifying glass on every action, intensifies the stakes of every split-second decision, making the difference between joyous triumph and gut-wrenching heartbreak.

Imagine the challenge of executing a pitstop within a tight window of 2-3 seconds. Such moments are where victory and defeat, separated by mere fractions on the track, are truly determined. And then there's the seemingly insignificant wheel nut. Many might overlook it, but in the high-pressure world of the pit lane, it has often been the difference between a race won and a race lost.

The relationship between the driver and the pit crew is built on profound trust. Every time the car halts in the pit box, that trust is palpable. Yet, instances of unsafe releases have tested this bond, putting a spotlight on the vulnerabilities that high-pressure scenarios can expose.

In the orchestrated chaos of the pit lane, where precision is paramount, even a single forgotten tool can be catastrophic, reflecting the thin line between safety and danger. Meanwhile, the ever-changing nature of race dynamics, be it due to a sudden rain shower or a strategic curveball, demands instantaneous decisions, each of which can redefine the course of the race.

But what truly makes Formula 1 enchanting is its inherent human touch. Despite the layers of technology and expertise, it's a sport vulnerable to human emotions, nerves, and errors. Recognizing this, understanding the dreams, the vulnerabilities, and the indomitable spirit of those who form the lifeblood of F1, deepens our appreciation and love for this incredible sport.

8

Depression in Formula 1

The mental well-being of Formula 1 drivers has assumed a paramount significance in recent years. There is now a heightened dedication from drivers, teams, and sponsors to allocate substantial resources towards assisting athletes in managing the substantial pressure and stress intrinsic to the sport. Despite numerous drivers candidly sharing their struggles, it is heartening to observe a perceptible reduction in the stigma surrounding mental health within motor sport. This progressive shift underscores the burgeoning awareness of the necessity to safeguard the psychological welfare of all involved.

Concurrently, teams, sponsors, and the sport itself have instigated comprehensive initiatives designed to provide improved guidance and support to drivers, with a particular emphasis on nurturing the mental fortitude of the younger generation. The foundation for this support begins at an early age, as evidenced by junior racing series such as Formula 4, which incorporates psychological testing and workshops into their curriculum.

These initiatives arm aspiring drivers with invaluable tools for developing resilience and emotional coping strategies requisite for excelling in a high-stakes environment. This holistic approach ensures that emerging talents are not only technically proficient but also adept at maintaining composure during competition.

In tandem with these endeavors, major sponsors have spear-headed their own initiatives to facilitate drivers' ability to manage the psychological rigors of the sport. An illustrative example is the 'Red Bull Racing Minds' initiative launched by Red Bull, a principal sponsor of the Red Bull Racing team, in 2017.

This pioneering program entails weekly meetings with psy-chologists, informative workshops on mental well-being, and the establishment of peer support groups. By fostering an environment where drivers can candidly share experiences and confront challenges collectively, these initiatives have delivered transformative benefits, especially for burgeoning talents.

The success story of Alex Albon, the current Williams driver, underscores the substantial impact of these support structures. Albon's inaugural year in Formula 1, while marked by adversity, culminated in him securing a full-time drive with Red Bull in 2020. His resilience and progress throughout this period were significantly bolstered by the support and psychological tools furnished by the Red Bull team. This anecdote underscores how Formula 1 is pioneering the integration of mental health support into the fabric of the sport.

Notably, the sport's governing body, the FIA, embarked on a vital mental health awareness campaign in 2020 to dismantle lingering stigma within the sport. This campaign encourages drivers to openly communicate their struggles and access available support services. It is further fortified by a rule mandating teams to provide ongoing psychological support throughout the season. This regulatory step underscores the sport's commitment to prioritize mental health and ensure that drivers can readily avail themselves of necessary assistance.

Crucially, individual drivers have played an instrumental role in bringing mental health to the forefront within motor sport. Eminent figures like Lewis Hamilton, Nico Rosberg, and Fernando Alonso have courageously shared their battles with depression and anxiety. Their narratives serve as potent testimonials to the power of resilience and seeking help when needed, dispelling any misguided notion that vulnerability equates to weakness.

The current era of Formula 1 imparts a heightened focus on preparing young drivers comprehensively. Initiatives that begin early in a driver's career, involving teams and sponsors investing in psychological support and equipping athletes with essential coping skills, serve as a paradigm for professional sports as a whole. The narratives of those who have triumphed over adversity are a source of inspiration not only within Formula 1 but also in the broader context of society.

Formula 1, despite its allure, remains a profession fraught with danger and potential fatality. With the advent of social media, the sport has witnessed a surge in pressure on drivers, exacerbating the risk of depression. Concurrently, accidents and fatalities on the track have raised pertinent questions regarding the balance between the sport's benefits and inherent dangers. Social media's pervasive influence, exerting pressure on drivers to conform to certain expectations, further compounds these mental health challenges. It is imperative to underscore that while Formula 1 offers exhilaration and rewards, the paramount concern should invariably be the safety and well-being of the drivers.

Depression, as a debilitating mental illness, exerts a profound impact on an individual's life. It encumbers their capacity to work, engage socially, and self-manage. In the crucible of Formula 1, where drivers face incessant pressure to excel, depression can emerge as a formidable adversary, impairing concentration, reflexes, and decision-making abilities. Furthermore, it jeopardizes relationships, engendering difficulty in establishing connections with others. Young drivers, ardently endeavoring to establish their presence on the grid, are especially susceptible to the deleterious effects of depression.

The emergence of social media as a potent influencer in Formula 1's narrative introduces an additional layer of complexity to drivers' mental health. While it facilitates interaction with fans and self-promotion, it can also catalyze stressors. Drivers often contend with intense scrutiny and criticism on these platforms, magnifying the psychological burden. Furthermore, social media fosters relentless comparisons among drivers, perpetuating feelings of inadequacy.

It is incumbent upon the sport to offer unwavering support and guidance to help drivers navigate these multifaceted pressures. Mental health professionals must be readily accessible to provide indispensable support and counsel. Teams should exhibit a heightened awareness of the potential mental health challenges their drivers may confront. Regulatory bodies should ensure that drivers possess the requisite resources and guidance to cope with the sport's formidable demands.

In summation, Formula 1 represents an intensely competitive domain where drivers confront formidable pressure to excel. This protracted strain necessitates a concerted effort from teams and governing bodies to prioritize the psychological well-being of drivers. The advent of social media has amplified these stressors, emphasizing the imperative for drivers to grasp the potential consequences of its usage. Depression and other mental health challenges, if unchecked, can imperil an individual's physical, emotional, and occupational spheres. Consequently, Formula 1 must not only preserve its electrifying allure but also remain committed to safeguarding the mental health of those who make the sport's glory possible.

Furthermore, it is pivotal to acknowledge Formula 1's historical backdrop, marred by tragic fatalities. With 225 recorded deaths in the annals of the sport, prudence dictates an unwavering commitment to prioritizing driver safety. This imperative extends to preserving and fortifying the mental well-being of those who partake in the high-stress environment of Formula 1. The initiatives undertaken, such as the FIA Action for Road Safety campaign, signal a resolute intent to champion mental health awareness within motor sport.

In conclusion, Formula 1, despite its allure and rewards, imposes colossal pressures on its drivers. These pressures are further exacerbated by the advent of social media. It is imperative for the sport to provide an extensive support network, emphasizing mental health awareness and offering resources to mitigate the challenges posed.

Acknowledging the paramount importance of mental health not only underscores Formula 1's commitment to holistic well-being but also sets an exemplary precedent for professional sports as a whole.

The narratives of resilience shared by those who have confronted mental health challenges serve as an enduring source of inspiration, resonating not only within the sport but also transcending its boundaries.

9

Depression's Ominous Shadow Over Formula 1's Young Stars

B ehind the glinting helmets and the blur of speed lie the beating hearts of Formula 1 drivers—young men and women*who, while mastering the laws of physics, often grapple with the intricate workings of their own minds.

The revelation by the National Institute of Mental Health, pointing to depression as a primary disability among adults between 18 and 25, paints a poignant picture of the internal battles these young racers might face, even as they navigate the hairpin turns of their illustrious profession.

Their ascent to the pinnacle of motor sport isn't just a story of unmatched skill and determination. It's also an intimate journey of dreams, aspirations, and at times, the haunting whispers of self-doubt. These emotional challenges, intensified by their inherent genetics, the monumental stress of the sport, and occasional trauma, coalesce into a formidable storm in the minds of these young drivers. Add to this, the intense magnification of public life and the persistent hum of expectations, and the landscape becomes even more challenging.

In today's interconnected world, a driver's life is not merely confined to the tarmac. The digital corridors of social media, while offering a platform for connection and a canvas for their personal narratives, also expose them to the less forgiving side of the internet. Moments of vulnerability, personal achievements, or even simple reflections, all become fodder for an audience that sometimes forgets the human soul behind the posts.

The dichotomy of the digital age is evident: as drivers share their highs and lows, the vast expanse of the internet amplifies love and support but also magnifies criticism, often crossing the line into undue negativity and even cruelty. It's a potent reminder that these champions, despite their larger-than-life personas on the track, carry the delicate emotions that are inherent to us all.

In our role as fans and observers, we don't just witness their breathtaking races; we're also privy to their emotional journeys. It's a privilege that comes with a responsibility—to celebrate, to commiserate, but always to empathize. Our words, whether of encouragement or critique, should never be wielded as weapons. There's no room in the Formula 1 community, or indeed in any community, for racism, harassment, or unbridled negativity.

Every podium, every setback, every lap is a testament to their physical prowess and mental fortitude. However, as we cheer for their overtakes or mourn their missed opportunities, it's imperative to remember the complex emotional landscape they navigate simultaneously.

Through the subsequent chapters, we'll journey deeper into their worlds, drawing inspiration from their triumphs and understanding from their challenges. Their tales aren't just about racing; they're about the resilience of the human spirit, facing adversities both visible on the track and invisible within.

*Is it permissible for women to compete in Formula 1?

Indeed, it is. There are no formal regulations in the sport that prevent women from taking part. However, several obstacles have historically hindered their consistent participation. It's notable that the most recent female to race in Formula One was Lella Lombardi, back in 1976.

Lella Lombardi, born Maria Grazia Lombardi on 26 March 1941, remains a significant figure in motor sport history. Hailing from Italy, Lella's passion and talent for racing led her to compete in 17 Grands Prix within the Formula One World Championship.

Her dedication and skill on the track were palpable, making her a role model for many aspiring racers.

Despite the challenges faced by women in a male-dominated sport during her era, Lella's determination saw her break barriers.

Lella Lombardi

10

Being a young driver in Formula 1

B eing a young Formula 1 driver is like waking up every morning on a rollercoaster that never stops. It's not just exhilarating; it's bewildering, complex, and sometimes just straight-up scary. Imagine yourself as a 21-year-old kid. You've got the dream job you've been working towards since you were eight, except now you realize it's not just about driving a car really fast.

Yeah, you're young, but your body's still a work-in-progress. While you're trying to manage your changing physique, you're also supposed to be in peak athletic shape. Every muscle twitch counts. And let's not even talk about how the travel messes with your sleep schedule. One week you're in the UK, the next you're in Singapore, and your internal body clock is basically like, "Dude, what the heck?"

You get homesick. Your mom's pasta, your dad's barbecue, hanging out with friends—you miss it all. And let's face it, even the fanciest hotel can feel like the loneliest place on earth when you're jet-lagged and can't sleep at 3 AM. You scroll through Instagram and see your friends hanging out, going to parties, or just chilling, and you can't help but feel isolated.

And oh boy, the media. They want to know everything, from your race strategies to your favorite color. One wrong answer, and Twitter will roast you alive. You're learning, but it feels like you're walking on eggshells all the time. You wish people understood that you're not just a brand or a soundbite, you're a human being with feelings and fears.

Yeah, you're famous now. But guess what? Fame is not just red carpets and champagne. It's paparazzi in your face when you're trying to grab a simple coffee. It's people you've never met having opinions about you. It's never knowing if someone likes you for you or because you're that hotshot F1 driver.

The paychecks and sponsorships are nice, but they come with their headaches. Suddenly, you're not just an athlete; you're a business. You have to worry about taxes, investments, and brand image. Balancing all these elements can mess with your head, and before you know it, you're googling symptoms of anxiety and depression.

To keep yourself grounded, you have to find your own little 'pit stops'—those moments of respite where you can just be yourself. Maybe you're into video games, or perhaps you've picked up meditation. You have to hold onto these things like a lifebuoy in the sea of constant expectations.

Here's something crucial: Don't be afraid to talk to a mental health professional. Sports culture has this macho vibe that shames people for seeking help, but screw that. You can be as tough as titanium but everyone has a breaking point. Therapy isn't a sign of weakness; it's the pit crew for your brain.

At the end of the day, you're not just an F1 driver. You're a young person navigating an incredibly complex landscape. It's okay to stumble, mess up, or even break down. You're learning, growing, and most importantly, you're living your dream—just remember to also take care of the person living it.

In the history of F1, there have been young drivers like Lewis Hamilton, Max Verstappen, and Charles Leclerc who've set incredible records, but they've also faced struggles that go beyond the race track. Daniel Ricciardo, who's known for his affable personality and contagious grin, didn't get there without navigating through trials of his own. Lando Norris might seem like the friendly guy-next-door on social media, but he's dealt with the constant pressure of being young and competitive. Mick Schumacher carries the enormous weight of his father's legendary name, all while trying to carve his own path in this demanding sport. These are the flesh-and-blood humans beneath the helmets.

The life of a young F1 driver is undeniably glamorous but equally grueling. It's a world where you're always on the clock, under scrutiny, and weighed down by the enormity of what you're trying to achieve. But if you can find the strength to steer through these challenges, not only will you emerge as a great driver, you'll be an even stronger person. So don't forget to take care of yourself—you're the most valuable player in your own life.

The life of a young Formula 1 driver is exhilarating but also relentlessly demanding. Imagine it like this: You're standing on a dizzying stage where the whole world seems to be judging your every move. Think of a pressure-cooker environment with the heat turned up to the max. The audience? Billions of eyes glued to screens, watching your every twist and turn. But it's not just the crowd you have to win; you've also got to beat legends who've been burning rubber for as long as you can remember.

Oh, it's not just about speed; you can't think that's all it takes. Ever tried doing a calculus problem while sprinting full speed?

That's kind of what it's like, except you're also navigating a fragile machine at insane speeds, wearing fire-resistant gear in sweltering heat. And let's not forget the sleepless nights from jet lag, hopping from one time zone to another. It's a grind—physically and mentally.

Add to that, you're always in the glare of media flashlights. Mess up a single word in an interview, and social media turns into a frenzied mob. There's no handbook on how to be perfect in public life; you're learning on the go. You have to be a good sport, a brand ambassador, a savvy communicator, and oh, also drive like the wind—all simultaneously.

Let's pause and talk about the fame and the bling. Imagine having all the sports cars you ever dreamed of but little time to drive them around for fun. Endorsements? Check. Money? Check. Privacy? Well, that's a luxury you can't afford. With fans and paparazzi tracking your every move, sometimes you might wonder if you're a person or a brand.

And God forbid you start having a series of bad races. The team grows restless. The sponsors get edgy. Every little error you make on the track becomes a big talking point. Your crew is working around the clock, but they're human too, and mistakes happen. The engine stalls, or tire strategies don't pan out. Suddenly, you're not just a driver; you're the focal point of a complex, multi-million-dollar operation. The weight of that is enormous.

Don't even get me started on the emotional roller coaster. You've got dreams and nightmares sharing the same mental space. The loneliness sets in during those long hotel nights. You miss your mom's cooking, your dad's jokes, and goofing around with your siblings or old friends. And when you're feeling low, there's no pit crew to fix that; you're your mechanic for your mind and soul.

So, what keeps you grounded? Your "me time" has to become sacred. Maybe you're listening to some chill music, nose deep in a novel, or laughing at a comedy skit. Exercise, but not the kind you do at the circuit—more like a jog through a quiet park or a quick yoga session. These moments help you re calibrate, and boy, you'll need plenty of that.

In this dog-eat-dog world, seeking professional help for your mental well-being isn't a sign of weakness; it's your shield. Whether it's a psychologist or a life coach, get someone in your corner. Trust me, it's not only allowed, it's essential.

I'll leave you with this: Yes, you've got engines to rev and races to win, but never forget that you're flesh and bones with a beating heart. You're not just a brand, a racer, or a star in the making. You're human, beautifully flawed and infinitely resilient.

Life in the Formula 1 lane? It's like dancing on a tightrope while juggling fire. Except here, you're not only the performer but also the choreographer, PR manager, and your own cheerleader. Welcome to the big leagues, kid. But remember, even in this high-stakes game, it's okay to take a pit stop for your soul.

Lewis Hamilton: Breaking Records, Breaking Norms

Lewis Hamilton was only 22 when he shot onto the F1 scene in 2007, capturing the world's attention by securing his first World Championship title a year later. The British driver has since amassed an astonishing seven World Championships, etching his name into the annals of the sport. But Hamilton isn't merely a driver; he's also a social activist and fashion icon, making him one of the most multifaceted figures in sports history.

Max Verstappen: The Wunderkind Grows Up

Max Verstappen was just a teenager—17 years old—when he burst into Formula 1 in 2015, setting records as the youngest driver ever to participate in the sport. His win at the 2016 Spanish Grand Prix not only affirmed his talent but made pundits rethink what young drivers could achieve. Max is known for his aggressive yet strategic driving, often making races electrifying from start to finish.

Red Bull Team

Charles Leclerc: The Ferrari Phenom

Charles Leclerc is one of those rare talents who seem destined for greatness. Making his F1 debut at the age of 20 in 2018, Leclerc quickly proved his worth. In 2019, he won his first Grand Prix and even outperformed his experienced Ferrari teammate, Sebastian Vettel. Leclerc isn't just about speed; he's about smarts—making calculated moves that often outwit his more experienced competitors.

Charles Leclerc - Ferrari Team

Lando Norris: The Rising Star with a Sense of Humor

Lando Norris - Mclaren Team

Lando Norris may be young, but he's already showing the kind of maturity that makes champions. Norris won the hearts of both traditional fans and a younger audience through his adept use of social media, providing humorous, behind-the-scenes glimpses into the often austere world of F1 racing. When he clinched his first podium in 2021, the Formula 1 community knew this was just a preview of what's to come.

Daniel Ricciardo: The Aussie With a Smile as Fast as His Car

Daniel Ricciardo's racing journey started far from the glamorous F1 tracks, in the dusty go-karting circuits of Perth, Australia. Ricciardo's charisma and famous "shoey" celebration make him an audience favorite, but it's his fearless overtaking and intelligent racing that have made him a respected figure in the paddock.

Daniel Riccardo - Mclaren Team

Mick Schumacher: The Weight and Privilege of a Name

Being Michael Schumacher's son brings a unique blend of pressure and opportunity, and Mick Schumacher knows it. The young German driver shows extraordinary dedication, seemingly drawing from his father's legacy while also determined to make his own mark. Despite the weight of expectations, he's shown signs of real talent, winning the FIA Formula 2 Championship and making a steady F1 debut with Haas in 2021.

Mick Shumacher - Haas Team

The life of a young F1 driver is far more complex than just turning wheels. Behind the visors and roaring engines are hours of grueling physical training, data analysis, and media obligations. They must navigate a sea of sponsorships and brand responsibilities, often while still learning the ropes of adulthood.

Being a digital native, this new generation of drivers also faces the joys and pitfalls of social media. Platforms like Twitter and Instagram serve as double-edged swords, offering immense visibility and personal connection with fans but at the risk of instant backlash for every perceived misstep.

In a sport as financially and emotionally taxing as Formula 1, young drivers face unprecedented challenges. They must not only hone their racing skills but also manage their brand, sustain public interest, and navigate complicated team dynamics—all while under immense public scrutiny.

Yet, this intense pressure cooker is where diamonds are made. The new breed of young drivers isn't just here to race; they're here to redefine what it means to be an F1 driver for a new generation. And in doing so, they carry the legacy of the sport into an exciting, unpredictable future.

Carlos Sainz is another name that has swiftly ascended in the Formula 1 hierarchy, leaving fans and pundits alike pleasantly surprised. Sainz, the son of rallying legend Carlos Sainz Sr., started his F1 journey with the Toro Rosso team back in 2015. Despite showing early promise, he had to bide his time in the midfield, driving for Renault and McLaren before getting his big break.

Carlos Sainz - Mclaren Team

In 2021, Sainz transitioned to Scuderia Ferrari, one of the most storied teams in F1 history, filling the shoes of four-time world champion Sebastian Vettel. This move was met with a mixture of anticipation and skepticism. But Sainz quickly dispelled any doubts with consistent performances and a superb ability to adapt to his new car. His first season with Ferrari saw him not just accumulating points but also forming a strong, synergistic partnership with teammate Charles Leclerc. This dynamic duo has been a silver lining in Ferrari's recent struggles, and the pair show promise of returning the team to its former glory.

Carlos Sainz isn't just another driver on the grid; he's a nuanced character who has mastered the art of resilience. His performances with Ferrari have shown he can handle the pressure that comes with a top-tier team. Sainz, often seen with a smile on his face, is a beloved figure in the paddock. He combines a light-hearted approach with a fiercely competitive spirit—a balance that has endeared him to fans and rivals alike.

Driving for Ferrari doesn't just mean being fast on the track; it means being an ambassador for a brand that symbolizes excellence, tradition, and passion. Carlos Sainz has seamlessly merged his identity with that of his team, embracing the pressure that comes with wearing the iconic red suit. From engaging with fans in multiple languages—showing off his linguistic talents—to exuding a passionate love for the sport, he personifies the modern F1 driver.

It's not just Sainz's driving that captures attention; it's his complete embodiment of the sport. He interacts with fans through well-curated social media channels, providing insights into the often intense life of an F1 driver. He shows the world what it means to work diligently behind the scenes: the strategic meetings, the tireless hours on the simulator, and the constant travel that shapes the life of an F1 star.

Sebastian Vettel, the four-time world champion, is often seen as a powerhouse in the world of Formula 1. His years of sheer dominance with Red Bull Racing from 2010 to 2013 won him a special place in the sport's annals. But the iconic driver, so poised and confident behind the wheel, has a side that's not always visible to the fans: the human side that grapples with emotional and mental complexities, just like any one of us.

Sebastian Vettel - Ferrari Team

After his transition to Ferrari, Sebastian found himself under a different kind of spotlight. The expectations at Ferrari are not just about winning; they're about carrying on a legacy. And that can be psychologically draining, even for the most seasoned drivers. The person we saw making rookie mistakes wasn't the Sebastian Vettel we were used to but someone under a kind of pressure that's hard to articulate.

Yet, in the face of adversity, Sebastian's human qualities—his humility, his thoughtful nature—came to the fore. He engaged deeply in charity work, spending time with children in hospitals, and remained an ever-dedicated family man. It's a testament to Sebastian's strong character that despite the mental toll, he never lost sight of what really mattered to him.

Fernando Alonso: A Phoenix Rising Again

Fernando Alonso is not just a Formula 1 driver; he's an institution. A two-time world champion, he's one of the most respected figures in motor sport. But even icons have their moments of vulnerability. Alonso's time at McLaren-Honda was emotionally taxing; the constant mechanical failures and lack of competitive edge were not easy for a man who lives to win. It took a toll on his mental health, challenging the reservoirs of resilience for which he was famous.

Fernando Alonso - Ferrari Team

But it's precisely this human aspect of Alonso—the ability to face struggles, take a step back, and then return with a rejuvenated spirit—that makes him so relatable and inspiring. During his time away from F1, he explored other racing series, even winning at Le Mans. It was a gentle reminder to himself and the world that he could still be a champion, that his talent was undiminished by adversity.

When he returned to F1 with Alpine, his love for the sport was palpable, as was his gratitude for a second chance to do what he loves.

His transparency about the challenges of coming back, both physical and mental, offered a window into the very human side of a sports superstar. Today, he uses his platform to engage with fans honestly and authentically, making him not just a great driver, but a true role model.

It's Okay Not to Be Okay

Both Sebastian and Fernando show us that it's perfectly human to face struggles and that it's okay not to be okay sometimes. Their experience is a critical reminder of the importance of mental health, even for those who seem invincible. The two champions may have faced difficulties, but they also found a way to heal and grow, both as athletes and as individuals.

It's a profound lesson for all of us—your struggles do not define you, but how you rise from them does. And in rising, both champions show us the remarkable strength and resilience of the human spirit. Their ongoing journeys are not just about laps and podiums but about conquering inner battles and discovering deeper aspects of themselves, which in many ways, is the most heroic feat of all.

11

The Ever-Evolving Landscape of
Formula 1 Teams

F ormula 1's tapestry is woven with tales of triumphs,
innovations, and legendary teams that have graced the
tracks since its birth in 1950. Each epoch has had its
heroes and its narratives, painting a vibrant panorama of motor
racing history.

In the dawn of Formula 1, it was the Italian maestros – Alfa
Romeo, Ferrari, and Maserati – that captured the imagination.
Alfa Romeo, with Giuseppe Farina in the cockpit, triumphed
in the first-ever championship.

And then there was Ferrari – a name that almost became
synonymous with the sport, whose roaring engines and red
cars came to epitomize Formula 1 passion. Maserati, though
not always in the limelight, added depth to this Italian romance
with the sport.

As the calendar pages turned to the 1960s, Britain rose to

prominence. Teams like British Racing Motors (BRM) and Lotus didn't just race; they revolutionized. Lotus, steered by the ingenious Colin Chapman, introduced novelties like the monocoque chassis and rear-engine designs. These weren't mere upgrades; they were transformative innovations.

Then came the era of McLaren and Williams in the 1970s and 80s. McLaren's journey, spearheaded by Ron Dennis, gave us heart-stopping moments with legends like Niki Lauda, Alain Prost, and Ayrton Senna. Williams, a brainchild of Sir Frank Williams, melded technical genius with the raw talent of drivers like Nigel Mansell and Damon Hill, capturing many podium finishes.

The turn of the century heralded what many fondly remember as the 'Schumacher Era'. The sheer brilliance of Michael Schumacher, coupled with Ferrari's expertise, painted many Sundays red, with a dominance rarely seen before.

In more recent times, Mercedes and Red Bull Racing have been the torchbearers. The silver arrows of Mercedes, helmed by talents like Lewis Hamilton, have been a dominant force. Red Bull, on the other hand, emerged as a relentless challenger, first with Sebastian Vettel's youthful exuberance and then with Max Verstappen's audacious drives.

But, as with any long-standing saga, there were evolutions and transformations. Teams have changed hands, names, and destinies. Who could forget the transition of Tyrrell to BAR, then Honda, followed by its metamorphosis into the championship-winning Brawn GP, and eventually evolving into the powerhouse that is Mercedes today? Similarly, teams like Renault, Jordan, Sauber, and Minardi have seen their destinies intertwined, reshaped, and reborn in various avatars, reflecting the sport's organic and dynamic nature.

Perhaps what stands out most poignantly is that Formula 1, while often celebrated for its drivers, is truly a tale of teams. Teams that have dreamt, teams that have innovated, and teams that have left an indelible mark on the asphalt of history. It's a world where engineering prowess meets human spirit, and where every turn of the wheel pens a chapter in a story that's still being written.

12

Michael Schumacher: The Maestro of Consistency and Precision

D ive into the heart of Formula 1's lore, and three names resonate deeply, echoing tales of courage, prowess, and sheer love for racing: Michael Schumacher, Ayrton Senna, and Niki Lauda. These aren't just names; they're legends who've woven their stories into the fabric of the sport, touching the souls of fans across the globe.

When I reflect on Michael Schumacher's journey in Formula 1, it isn't just the roaring engines or the breathtaking overtakes that resonate; it's the unmistakable essence of a man so deeply connected to his passion. To the world, "Schumi" was an unmatched maestro of speed and strategy. But for those who looked a little closer, he represented so much more.

From his early days in 1991, Michael exuded a raw, palpable connection with racing. You could see it in the way he communicated with his car, coaxing out performances that left audiences worldwide in sheer awe.

It was almost like they were partners in a breathtaking dance, one that earned them seven world titles. But those titles, as magnificent as they are, only scratch the surface of who Michael was.

Behind the helmet was a deeply dedicated individual. Those countless hours spent in the garage, the tireless days of testing, the seemingly endless debrief sessions – they all paint a picture of a man profoundly committed not just to winning but to the spirit of the sport. His relationships with his teams, whether it was Benetton or the iconic Ferrari, felt familial. He wasn't just a driver; he was a brother, a mentor, a cornerstone of their collective dream.

And who can forget his epic battles? Duels with legends like Damon Hill and Mika Häkkinen weren't just about points and podiums. They were glimpses into Michael's heart, showcasing his unwavering determination, his fiery spirit, and a competitive nature that was always balanced with respect for his fellow racers.

Yet, it was during moments of challenge that Michael's true character shone the brightest. The 1999 crash at the British Grand Prix wasn't just a test of his physical strength, but a testament to his resilience and spirit. Watching him climb back, with that same trademark determination, was like witnessing the human spirit in its purest form.

To me, Michael Schumacher is more than a racing icon. He's an embodiment of dedication, of passion, and of the relentless pursuit of dreams. His story isn't just about the tracks he conquered but about the hearts he touched and the indelible mark he left on the sport and its admirers.

Michael remains with us, and I choose to celebrate him as the living legend he truly is.

13

Ayrton Senna: The Artist of Speed and Passion

W hen I think of Ayrton Senna, the first word that comes to my mind is passion. This Brazilian maestro wasn't just another racer; he was a force of nature. From the moment he stepped onto the track, you could feel that every inch of his being was immersed in the act of racing. There was an undeniable magnetism about him – it was hard to look away.

Hailing from São Paulo, Brazil, Senna's love affair with racing began in the world of karting. It was evident from the get-go that he was no ordinary driver. His flair, his raw speed, and his visceral connection to his machine made him an instant sensation.

What endeared Senna to me, and so many others, was not just his prodigious talent but his genuine humanity. He wore his heart on his sleeve, and this was evident every time he was behind the wheel. His eyes, so intensely focused, told stories of his dreams, his challenges, and his unyielding spirit.

His battles on the racetrack, especially with fierce competitors like Alain Prost, are stuff legends are made of. Their duels were electrifying, as two of the sport's titans clashed with unmatched intensity. Senna's legendary laps in the rain, particularly at Donington in 1993, were sheer poetry in motion, a dance between man and machine, unified against the elements.

Ayrton Senna Bronze Statue in Rio de Janeiro

Beyond the track, Senna's dedication to his home country and his deep sense of spirituality added layers to his personality. He was known for his charity work and always expressed a profound connection to the people of Brazil. In his victories, he didn't just race for himself, but for every Brazilian who saw in him a beacon of hope and inspiration.

Tragically, the world lost Senna far too soon in the ill-fated 1994 San Marino Grand Prix. Yet, his legacy remains intact, shining brightly like a star that refuses to fade. In his life, he touched countless souls with his talent, passion, and humanity.

14

Niki Lauda

N iki Lauda, whose full name was Andreas Nikolaus
Lauda, was a legendary Austrian Formula One driver
and a prominent figure in the motor sport world.
Born on February 22, 1949, in Vienna, Austria, and passing
away on May 20, 2019, Lauda's life and career were marked by
incredible achievements, remarkable resilience, and a profound
impact on the sport.

Lauda's Formula One journey began in the early 1970s when
he made his debut in 1971 with the March team before moving
on to BRM and then Ferrari. It was during his time with
Scuderia Ferrari that Lauda achieved his greatest success.
In the 1975 Formula One season, he won his first World
Drivers' Championship title with Ferrari. His disciplined and
methodical approach to racing earned him the nickname "The
Computer" within the racing community.

However, it was the 1976 Formula One season that defined
Lauda's career and showcased his incredible determination.

During the German Grand Prix at the Nürburgring, Lauda suffered a horrific accident, crashing and being trapped in his burning car. Despite his life-threatening injuries, including severe burns to his face and lungs, he remarkably returned to racing just six weeks later, showing unparalleled courage and tenacity. Although he narrowly lost the championship to James Hunt that year, his recovery and comeback remain one of the most inspiring stories in motor sport history.

Lauda's rivalry with James Hunt became the stuff of legend, and their contrasting personalities and driving styles added drama and excitement to Formula One during that era. Their intense battles on the track and mutual respect off it captivated fans around the world.

Niki Lauda continued to race in Formula One and won his second World Championship with Ferrari in 1977. He eventually retired from racing in 1979 but returned to the sport with McLaren in 1982. In his third and final championship-winning season in 1984, he secured his third title, firmly establishing his status as one of the sport's great champions.

Lauda was not only known for his racing prowess but also for his outspoken and straightforward personality. After retiring from racing, he transitioned to various roles in the motor sport world, including team management. He played a pivotal role in Mercedes' return to Formula One as a works team and their subsequent dominance in the hybrid era.

Beyond his contributions to Formula One, Lauda was a successful businessman, founding Lauda Air, an airline company, and was involved in various aviation-related ventures.

Tragically, Niki Lauda passed away in 2019 at the age of 70, leaving behind a lasting legacy in the world of motor sport. He remains an enduring symbol of courage, determination, and excellence in the face of adversity, and his name will forever be associated with one of the most remarkable comebacks in sports history.

Niki Lauda

To me, the narratives of Schumacher, Senna, and Lauda go beyond mere tales of three racers.

They symbolize passion, resilience, and the very essence of what it means to chase a dream.

When I think of them, I'm reminded of the boundless potential within all of us, waiting to be unlocked.

Their names continue to evoke a sense of awe and inspiration, reminding us of the passion, skill, and dedication that define Formula 1 at its highest level.

15

Lewis Hamilton: More Than a Champion

L ewis Hamilton isn't just one of my favorite driver because he's a genius on the racetrack. Sure, the thrill of watching him cut corners with precision and speed to the finish line is beyond exciting. But what really draws me to Lewis is something much deeper—it's his willingness to show that he's human, just like all of us.

He talks openly about his mental health, about battling depression, and let me tell you, that's a breath of fresh air in a sport that often feels like it's all about appearing invincible. When Lewis shares his own struggles, it's as if he's pulling you aside and saying, "Hey, it's okay not to be okay." And that's huge.

It's revolutionary in a world where drivers are often put on pedestals as if they're superheroes who are immune to real-life problems.

Listening to him discuss the emotional toll of racing, you can feel that he's not just ticking off talking points; he's sharing a piece of his soul. He speaks with a kind of sincerity that leaves a lump in your throat because you can sense how real and close to home these issues are for him. When he talks about mental health, he gives a voice to a silent struggle that many people—including myself—know all too well but seldom discuss openly.

His concern for safety in the sport also feels deeply genuine. I sense that his push for better safety isn't just for the sake of regulations. He's looking out for his peers, and that quality shows that his compassion extends beyond his own challenges and concerns. His advocacy makes me feel like he's not just racing for himself but for everyone involved in the sport. And that speaks volumes about his character.

But the moments that really melt my heart? When he talks about his family. His voice softens, his eyes light up, and you can tell how much they mean to him. It's like the racing champion facade slips away for a moment, and you're left with Lewis the son, the brother, the family man. These glimpses of the real Lewis remind us all that he's not just a machine programmed to win races; he's a person who loves and is loved deeply by his family.

So, for me, Lewis Hamilton is so much more than a legendary racer. He's a hero, but not for the reasons you might expect.

He's a hero because he's not afraid to show that he's human.

He gives us permission to talk about our struggles and faces his own openly and honestly. In a sport that's so often about chasing time, Lewis makes the time to talk about what truly matter.

Lewis Hamilton

16

The trauma

The trauma of crashes and injuries can contribute to depression in Formula 1 in a number of ways. Many of the drivers in Formula 1 have experienced some form of traumatic event while racing, whether it be a crash or an injury, and this can have long-term psychological impacts on the drivers. This trauma can lead to depression, anxiety, and other forms of mental health issues, which can have a major impact on drivers' performance on the track.

Firstly, a crash or injury can lead to post-traumatic stress disorder (PTSD). This disorder can develop when someone experiences a traumatic event, such as a crash or injury. PTSD can be characterized by flashbacks, nightmares, and intrusive thoughts, which can be extremely distressing for the individual. In the case of Formula 1 drivers, these flashbacks and intrusive thoughts can be very disruptive to their mental health, as they are constantly being re-exposed to the traumatic events that they experienced while racing. Additionally, drivers may also experience feelings of guilt and shame, as they may feel as though they could have done something differently to avoid the crash or injury. This can be very damaging for their mental health and may lead to depression.

Secondly, an injury or crash can also lead to physical pain. Pain can have a major psychological impact, as it can lead to feelings of helplessness and hopelessness, which can further contribute to depression. In the case of Formula 1 drivers, the physical pain that they may experience from their injuries can be both physically and psychologically damaging, as it can affect their ability to perform on the track. Additionally, drivers may also experience emotional pain from the trauma of their injury, as this can lead to feelings of sadness, grief and loss. This can be a major contributing factor to depression in Formula 1 drivers.

Finally, a crash or injury can lead to fear of future crashes or injuries. This fear can be extremely debilitating and can lead to feelings of anxiety and depression. In the case of Formula 1 drivers, this fear can be particularly damaging, as they may be more likely to take risks or make mistakes in order to avoid a crash or injury. This fear can also lead to a loss of motivation and a decrease in performance, which can further contribute to depression in Formula 1 drivers.

Overall, the trauma of crashes and injuries can have a major impact on the mental health of Formula 1 drivers. The trauma of a crash or injury can lead to post-traumatic stress disorder, physical pain, and fear of future crashes or injuries, all of which can contribute to depression in Formula 1 drivers. It is therefore important that drivers receive the necessary support and treatment to help them manage the psychological impacts of their trauma so that they can perform at their best on the track.

17

Within the realm of Formula 1...

When I look at Formula 1, beyond the roaring engines and the shimmering cars, I see a world deeply human at its core. It's a spectacle that I've admired, not just for its thrilling races but for the passionate souls that make it all come alive.

Being a fan, I've often felt the adrenaline, the highs and lows with every race. But what truly resonates with me is the profound humanity behind those visors and steering wheels. Think about it – these drivers, though they seem almost superhuman at times, grapple with the immense weight of expectations.

Each race isn't just a quest for a podium finish but a relentless battle to prove their worth. For them, every twist and turn on the track mirrors the unpredictability of life, the challenges of staying at the top, and the fear of fading into obscurity.

Away from the spotlight, there's a side to their lives that many don't see. The ceaseless scrutiny, the media's glare, and the constant tug-of-war between personal and public lives. Sometimes, I wonder how they cope with it all. How they manage to smile for the cameras when their every move is dissected, or how they handle the pressure of being ambassadors for so many brands and causes.

And then there's the unspoken challenge of finances. The world of Formula 1 isn't just about talent; it's intrinsically tied to money. The anxiety of ensuring that they remain valuable to their teams, that they justify their place both with performance and the financial muscle they bring – it's a balance that must be incredibly hard to maintain.

Beyond these obvious pressures, there's the toll the sport takes on their personal lives. The incessant travel, the physical exhaustion, the sacrifices they make in personal relationships – it paints a picture of isolation, even amidst the buzz of the paddock.

At the end of the day, when I reflect on why I'm so drawn to Formula 1, it's these human stories that touch me the most.

Because beneath the helmets and the fame, these drivers are people, with dreams, fears, and vulnerabilities. And it's a reminder that even in the fast-paced world of F1, there's a heartbeat, a raw and profound human essence, that we must always cherish and support.

18

The pinnacle of motor sport

Diving deep into the world of Formula 1, I often find myself lost in a whirlwind of emotions. Yes, it's about speed, precision, and the awe-inspiring roar of engines. But if you peer just a bit closer, it's so much more. It's about the heartbeats behind the helmets, the tireless teams in the pit, and the sheer weight of hopes and dreams they all carry on their shoulders.

Every time an F1 driver slides into their cockpit, they're not just strapping into a machine; they're committing themselves to a dance with gravity. The gut-wrenching G-forces, the intense concentration to navigate at breakneck speeds - it's a physical and mental marathon. And just as their muscles scream in protest with every sharp turn, their hearts and minds are in a race of their own. But it's not a solo journey. Behind every driver, there's a team, training alongside them, feeling every bump and turn, sharing in every strain and stretch. They too endure sleepless nights and exhaustive schedules to ensure everything is primed to perfection.

But, amidst this dizzying world of speed and strategy, lies a silent, often overlooked adversary: the weight of mental health challenges.

The pressure to be consistently flawless, the knowledge that every split-second decision has consequences, can cast a heavy shadow. A driver's mind is their most potent tool, but the constant scrutiny, the weight of a nation's or a sponsor's hopes, can sometimes lead to crippling self-doubt. And it's not just them. The engineers, the strategists, the support crew - they all grapple with the relentless pressure to be the best, every single time. A missed calculation, a delayed pit stop, even by a fraction of a second, and it all comes crashing down.

The nature of the sport, with its constant travel and isolation from loved ones, only adds another layer. It's a life where hotel rooms often become a sanctuary, where one can momentarily escape the blinding spotlight. For many, this life on the move can breed feelings of loneliness, making them question their purpose, their worth. This emotional toll, though not often spoken about, is as real and challenging as any physical injury.

Formula 1, for me, is more than just a sport. It's a window into the complexities of the human spirit. Every race is a testament to human resilience, dedication, and the battles both seen and unseen. It reminds me that behind the glam and glitter, these are real people with real struggles.

It's a world where victories are celebrated, but it's also essential to remember and support the drivers and teams during the more challenging moments, to ensure that no one faces their battles alone.

19

Formula 1 History unfold as a rich tapestry

F ormula 1, as I've keenly observed over the years, is
more than just high-speed races on tarmac ribbons
worldwide. It's an ever-evolving narrative, driven by
passion, rivalry, and immense ambition. When I recount the
sheer intensity of the tussles between Ayrton Senna and Alain
Prost, especially the 1989 Japanese Grand Prix showdown, it's
almost palpable—the way these two titans clashed, epitomizing
a raw competitive spirit that has always been the essence of F1.

While individual rivalries have often grabbed headlines, the dynamics between powerhouse teams like Ferrari and McLaren in
the late '90s have given fans much to debate. The strategies, the
tech wars, the claims of espionage, and the mutual allegations
added layers of complexity to the already high-stakes world of
F1.

However, as much as I am enamored by the thrilling on-track

action and behind-the-scenes politics, I've become increasingly concerned about the unspoken challenges. As we ushered into the digital era and social media started to dominate the discourse, I noticed the magnified spotlight on everyone in the F1 circus. Drivers, once insulated by the boundaries of traditional media, found themselves thrust under an unrelenting microscope, with every move dissected by fans and critics alike in real-time.

With this exposure came the inevitable emotional and mental repercussions. Several drivers, young and old, began sharing their battles with depression, anxiety, and other mental health issues. Take the young drivers, for instance, who enter the sport filled with dreams and face the dual pressure of immediate results and immense online scrutiny. The relentless nature of social media means that a single mistake in a race can result in a barrage of criticism, memes, and even personal attacks, which can be incredibly overwhelming.

Some drivers have opened up about the sleepless nights, the self-doubt, and the emotional strain that come with the job. Not to forget, the inherent danger of the sport itself is an ever-present psychological burden. Every time they strap into their machines, they're aware of the risks involved. This juxtaposed with the need to be "perfect" for fans, sponsors, and their teams can be mentally daunting.

The teams aren't immune either. The people behind the scenes, from the strategists to the engineers, face their own set of challenges. The blame for a poor strategy call or a mechanical failure can lead to online backlash. In an era where information travels at lightning speed, protecting one's mental well-being has become paramount.

I've realized, with a heavy heart, that while technology and social media have revolutionized fan engagement and brought us closer to the sport we love, they have also added a new dimension of challenges for those who make F1 the spectacle it is. It underscores the importance of mental health awareness and the need for support structures within the sport. To me, it's a poignant reminder that our heroes, in their blazing fast machines, are humans after all – grappling with vulnerabilities just like the rest of us.

Formula 1, with its pulsating pace and intricate strategies, has given us moments that linger in our memories, not just for the spectacle they provide but for the deeply human emotions they stir.

The 1997 European Grand Prix stands out as a vivid canvas of emotions and ambitions. The climactic encounter between Michael Schumacher and Jacques Villeneuve wasn't merely a racing incident; it was a confluence of aspirations and dreams. The fallout, which saw Schumacher disqualified, reflected not just the stakes of the sport but the depths of passion these athletes harbor. It was a reminder that beneath the helmets and fireproof suits, there lie beating hearts driven by an undying quest for glory.

The 2002 Austrian Grand Prix brought to the forefront a complex tapestry of team dynamics and personal ambitions. The decision for Rubens Barrichello to allow Michael Schumacher to take the lead wasn't just about points and podiums; it was about sacrifice, loyalty, and the sometimes heart-wrenching choices that come with being part of a larger mission.

The 2010 German Grand Prix illustrated the intense rivalries that can brew within the confines of the racetrack. The duel between Fernando Alonso and Lewis Hamilton, culminating in a fateful collision, was more than just a racing incident. It was a testament to the fragile balance between individual pursuit and collective team dynamics.

Then there's the 2012 Brazilian Grand Prix, where Sebastian Vettel's decision to overtake teammate Mark Webber echoed the intricate interplay of personal ambitions and team cohesion. Vettel's move wasn't just about the thrill of the chase; it touched upon the subtle nuances of teamwork and the challenges of managing individual aspirations within a collective framework.

Such moments serve as poignant reminders that Formula 1 isn't just about speed and strategy. It's a realm where human emotions, ambitions, and bonds play out against the backdrop of roaring engines and blazing tarmac. Each race, each lap, and each turn encapsulates the dreams and dilemmas of individuals striving for personal and collective greatness.

20

The Future of Formula 1 and Depression

Reflecting on the heart-pounding exhilaration that Formula 1 brings to fans, I can't help but think of the roller coaster ride of emotions the drivers themselves go through. While it's easy to be captivated by the glamour, glitz, and high-octane action of the sport, beneath the helmet lies a human being who grapples with an array of intense emotions.

In recent conversations with friends and fellow enthusiasts, the burning question that often emerges is about the future of F1. With a shifting global perspective towards sustainability and growing concerns over environmental issues, there's no doubt the sport needs to pivot. But it's more than just addressing the carbon footprint or fuel alternatives; there's a more profound human element at play here.

Now, juxtaposing this with the high-intensity, high-pressure environment of F1, it's alarming but perhaps not surprising that a significant portion of these gladiators on the track experience symptoms of depression.

The sheer mental toll, along with the physical demands, is something hard to fathom for us as mere spectators. The gladiatorial image, the roaring engines, and the glint of the championship trophy often overshadow the very real, raw, and vulnerable side of these athletes.

Imagine, then, being a Formula 1 driver. You're constantly in the limelight, scrutinized for every move, every decision. The pressure to perform, to be the best, to constantly innovate and push your limits - it's relentless. And this is just the tip of the iceberg. The financial strain, sponsor commitments, media duties, not to mention the looming risk every time they strap into that car. The sense of isolation can be profound, especially when the general perception is that these drivers live the dream. The fear of opening up, of being seen as weak, can further exacerbate feelings of loneliness and depression.

Formula 1, as it stands at the precipice of the future, has an obligation. Beyond technological advances and eco-conscious shifts, the sport must prioritize its drivers' well-being, both physically and mentally. There needs to be a space for dialogue, an environment where mental health isn't stigmatized but rather acknowledged and addressed. Teams need to rally around not just the athlete, but the person behind the visor. Resources, counselors, support systems - these should be as integral to F1 as the pit crew or the strategists.

In charting out the course for the future, it's high time the sport looked inward. Sustainable practices, technology, and safety measures are crucial, no doubt. But at the heart of it all, the well-being of the drivers, the very soul of the sport, cannot be sidelined.

In conversations at the local cafe or heated debates on online forums, while we speculate on the next big champion or dissect the latest race strategies, let's also pause. Let's remember the human element, appreciate the sacrifices, and hope that as Formula 1 hurtles into the future, it does so with the well-being of its drivers firmly in the driver's seat.

As I sat scrolling through my Instangram feed, sipping my morning coffee, I stumbled upon an image of an F1 driver I've admired for years.

With the backdrop of a beautiful sunset, he wrote, "Even in the midst of the storm, the sun still shines."

The post was cryptic but hinted at an underlying battle he might be facing. I felt a sudden pang of concern but also wondered how many others recognized the subtext behind that serene image.

Social media, in all its glory, is a double-edged sword. While it has bridged the gap between fans and their sporting heroes, it's also thrown open a window into their vulnerabilities.

With #mentalhealth trending across platforms and many celebrities openly discussing their struggles, it's hardly surprising that the fast-paced, high-pressure world of Formula 1 isn't immune to these very human challenges.

The echoing roar of engines, the adrenaline rush of overtakes, the strategy games that play out on the asphalt— all these can easily make us forget the pressures faced by the very men and women behind those visors. The rigorous travel, the media glare, the weight of team and sponsor expectations, not to mention the inherent risks every time they step onto the track. While their Instagram might showcase champagne showers and glamorous after-parties, who truly knows the weight of the helmet they put on, both literally and metaphorically?

As fans, our role in this digital age is more significant than we realize. We wield more power with our words and reactions than ever before. A single tweet can create ripples. A supportive comment on an Instagram post can lift spirits. But the converse is equally, if not more, impactful. Hasty judgments, unkind memes, and the cacophony of negativity can deepen the wounds of someone already grappling with internal battles.

So, how should we navigate this?

Empathy Over Judgment: Before hitting 'send' on that snarky tweet or critical comment, pause. Reflect. Would you say this if you were face to face with them?

Understanding and kindness go a long way.

Educate Ourselves: Just as we invest time in understanding the technicalities of the sport, why not delve into the mental aspect of it?

Recognizing signs, understanding challenges, and being aware can lead to a more supportive environment.

Promote Positive Conversations: It's easy to join the bandwagon of negativity. It takes courage to steer conversations towards understanding and support.

Encourage fan forums, groups, and fellow enthusiasts to foster a culture of respect.

Respect Boundaries: Everyone, including our sporting heroes, needs their space.

Understand that while they share snippets of their lives with us, they don't owe us every detail.

Lend Support: Be it positive comments, support campaigns, or even joining groups that promote mental well-being, every little bit helps.

In the world of Formula 1, as engines rev and races are won, we, the audience, play a pivotal role. Beyond being mere spectators, we're a part of the ecosystem that can either elevate or erode the mental well-being of those we admire.

Let's choose our roles wisely, bearing in mind the power of the digital age and the depth of human vulnerability.

21

Formula 1 # we race as one

In the high-speed world of Formula 1, it's easy to get caught up in the excitement of roaring engines and fierce rivalries. But amidst the thunderous applause and adrenaline-pumping action, let's not forget that the sport isn't just about cars and checkered flags; it's about people.

The drivers who push the boundaries of human capability, who risk it all for their passion, aren't machines. They're athletes, dreamers, and daredevils with hearts that beat just like ours. They feel the thrill of victory and the sting of defeat. They share our joy and our pain.

So, as fans of this incredible sport, let's stick together and help Formula 1 grow in a healthy environment. Let's remember that our support and passion can make a difference, not just in the spectacle of the races but also in the lives of those who make it all possible.

Let's cheer for the underdogs, respect the champions, and

applaud the unsung heroes behind the scenes. Let's celebrate the victories, but also show empathy in defeat.

Formula 1 is not just about the cars on the track; it's a community of enthusiasts, united by a shared love for speed, skill, and the pursuit of excellence.

Together, we can create an environment where the sport thrives, where drivers are not just seen as icons but as individuals with dreams and feelings.

Together, we can keep the spirit of Formula 1 alive and roaring, inspiring generations to come.

So, let's rev up our support, remember the human side of the sport, and drive Formula 1 to greater heights, always with respect, sportsmanship, and a love for the thrill of the race.

we race as one

22

Conclusion

In conclusion, as fans of Formula 1, our role extends beyond mere spectators. We are an integral component of the sport's ecosystem, and our actions, both online and offline, have a significant impact.

By supporting teams and drivers with respect, empathy, and understanding, we not only promote a healthier environment but also contribute to the mental well-being of the individuals who give their all for our entertainment. Engaging positively on social media, discouraging negativity and trolling, and appreciating the hard work and dedication of all involved, irrespective of race outcomes, can create a nurturing atmosphere. Moreover, attending races, buying merchandise, and supporting sponsors are tangible ways to bolster the sport economically.

We must remember that Formula 1 thrives not just on the performances on the track but also on the community spirit off it.

As fans, our united front can significantly help in driving the sport forward, ensuring that both teams and drivers feel valued, appreciated, and supported in their endeavors.

Epilogue

Epilogue: Reflections in the Rear view Mirror

As the final pages of "The Dark Side Behind the Wheel" turn, we're left peering into the intricate, oft-ignored world of Formula 1 – a world not just of roaring engines and dazzling speeds, but of human beings vulnerable to the same societal pressures as the rest of us. The grandeur and glamour of the F1 circus can easily overshadow the more subtle battles being waged off the track: those of the mind and soul.

Social media, with its unfiltered access and relentless immediacy, has become a double-edged sword. While it offers fans unprecedented insights and connections to their sporting heroes, it also throws open the floodgates to a torrent of criticism, negativity, and, at times, unwarranted cruelty.

Each tweet, comment, or post, no matter how thoughtlessly typed out in a moment of passion, can lodge like a shard in the psyche of its recipient. For an F1 driver or team member, whose professional life is a constant quest for perfection, these digital darts can exacerbate anxieties, cloud judgments, and even erode confidence.

By delving deep into the shadows of the sport, we've not

only exposed the vulnerabilities of its participants but also highlighted the responsibilities of its followers. Every fan, blogger, or journalist holds a share of power in shaping the mental landscapes of those they admire.

In the future, as the engines fire up for another season and the world tunes in to watch these gladiators of the track, let's hope "The Dark Side Behind the Wheel" serves as a reminder – a beacon of empathy and compassion. For in celebrating the sport's triumphs, we must also safeguard the spirits of those who make it all possible.

The race isn't just won on the asphalt; it's also in the hearts and minds of everyone involved. As fans, critics, and enthusiasts, the wheel is in our hands too.

Let's steer the narrative towards understanding, respect, and unity.

For in the end, the true essence of Formula 1 lies not in the machines but in the humans behind them.

Teams and Drivers

Afterword

Afterword: Through My Eyes

In the vast tapestry of opinions and perspectives, every thread has its own unique shade, its own narrative. "The Dark Side Behind the Wheel" is one such thread, colored by my personal experiences, emotions, and beliefs. It's true, not everyone will align with the way I perceive Formula 1. Some might accuse me of partiality towards certain drivers or teams, while others may simply dismiss my viewpoints. And that's perfectly alright.

It's essential to remember that this book is an embodiment of my perspectives and feelings. It's the way I've seen and interpreted events, the way emotions have swelled up inside me during races, and the lessons I've drawn from those experiences. And just as I respect diverse views, I hope readers understand that this is my unique lens, my singular voice amidst the multitude.

It's worth clarifying that I stand staunchly against any form of prejudice – be it racism, bullying, or any other manifestation of intolerance and violence. Such behaviors have no place in my world or the world I wish for others.

This book was born from a desire to celebrate the drivers

who've paved the way, to learn from their journeys, and to kindle positive change. I envisioned it as a beacon, urging fans and readers to harness the power of social media responsibly, constructively. Not just for the betterment of Formula 1 drivers and their teams, but for athletes and individuals across all arenas and corners of the globe.

In the era of hashtags and trending topics, I hope that we choose our words wisely, craft narratives that uplift, and support endeavors that build bridges rather than walls.

Thank you for embarking on this journey with me, for listening to my story, and hopefully, for being a part of the positive change that I aspire to inspire.

Milton Keynes UK
Ingram Content Group UK Ltd.
UKHW020214141023
430515UK00010B/58

9 798210 875570